# Kitchens

ROCKPORT

# Kitchens

GLOUCESTER MASSACHUSETTS

ROCKPORT PUBLISHERS

Texts: Marina Ubach
Graphic Design: Emma Termes Parera
Layout: Gisela Legares Gili

Copyright for the international edition:
© H Kliczkowski-Onlybook, S.L.
La Fundición, 15. Polígono Industrial Santa Ana
28529 Rivas-Vaciamadrid. Madrid
Ph.: +34 91 666 50 01
Fax: +34 91 301 26 83
asppan@asppan.com
www.onlybook.com

Copyright for the US edition:
© 2004 by Rockport Publishers, Inc.

Published in the United States of America by
Rockport Publishers, Inc.
33 Commercial Street
Gloucester, Massachusetts 01930-5089
Tel.: (978) 282-9590
Fax: (978) 283-2742
www.rockpub.com

Library of Congress Cataloging-in-Publication Data available
ISBN: 1-59253-058-3

10 9 8 7 6 5 4 3 2 1

Printed in Singapore

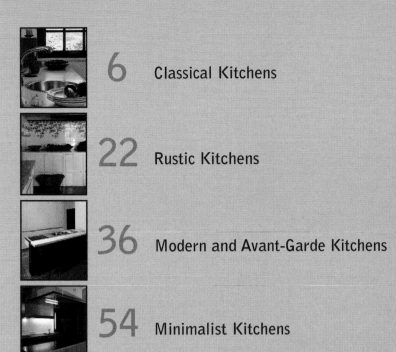

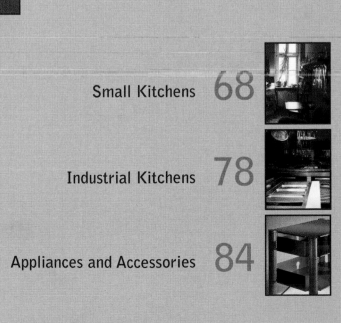

Classical-style kitchens are defined by their precise aesthetic with paneled cabinets in the upper and lower parts of the work zone. Light-toned woods help to re-create a style which respects tradition. It is important not to overload the area, since the kitchen should be, above all, a very practical and comfortable space so as to be able to work freely. Solid wood cabinets may be elected, though veneered furnishings are more common in kitchens given the fact that they are lighter and more economical. Nowadays, purely classical cabinets with an elegant aesthetic are manufactured, though more contemporary designs may also be included in this style. Among these types of kitchens, the ones that utilize very innovative materials stand out for the incorporation of very light-colored materials (e.g., white veneers and laminations) or combined with glass. Cabinets with shelves and glass enhance this style, as do paneled doors. Coverings for floors and walls are very useful in defining the classical style of a kitchen. The use of light-toned wooden slats for floor surfaces and ceramic tiles for walls offer very good results. A marble or granite countertop gives the work zone a classical and elegant appearance. Classical sinks, fixtures, and extractor hoods highlight this style, as do refined appliances. Light materials are good for the utility room, the walls of which may be painted with light colors or covered with wallpaper. Even decorative friezes are an option.

Photography: José Luis Hausmann

Photography: Montse Garriga

Photography: José Luis Hausmann

Photography: José Luis Hausmann

Photography: José Luis Hausmann

Photography: José Luis Hausmann

Photography: Nuria Fuentes

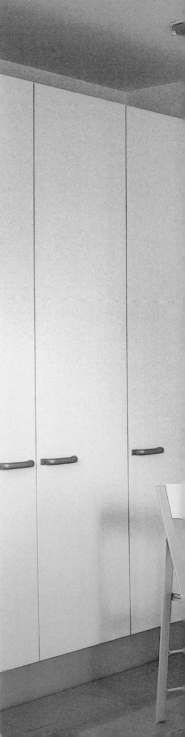

Rustic kitchens recreate a rural and natural living style. Solid wood fittings in natural colors or darker tones are most appropriate for this type of kitchen, though veneered fittings are used more often nowadays. Also appropriate are furnishings painted blue, white, and green. Rustic cabinet doors include panels covered in wood, glass, or chicken wire. Another good option is work pieces in the lower areas of the kitchen, typical in rural homes, which may be decorated with restored doors or checkered curtains with flounces. With regard to coverings, good ideas for the walls are utilizing white ceramic tile, restoring stone or brick walls, or applying paints that offer an irregular finish. Old-style kitchens in which half of the wall was tiled so as to cover the work zone (the area exposed to the most wear and tear) and the rest painted may also be imitated. For floors, clay tiles or wide wooden slats are ideal. Restored wooden beams, even painted, are good for ceilings. There is a variety of antique furniture that fits in perfectly with this type of kitchen: work tables (large tables used to prepare meals), auction cupboards (large glass cupboards to store crockery), brass handles or old fixtures that can be combined with porcelain details. Today, many kitchens combine antique elements and cutting edge fittings with aesthetically pleasing results. Details such as old decorative guides with saucepans and pans, shelves with spice bottles, or wicker boxes contribute to achieving the necessary warmth.

Photography: Jordi Miralles

Photography: Jordi Miralles

Photography: Jordi Miralles

Photography: José Luis Hausmann

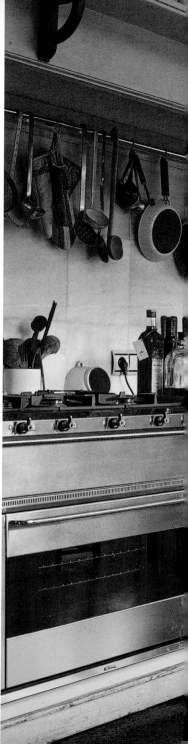

Photography: José Luis Hausmann

Photography: Jordi Miralles

These are the most up-to-date kitchens, with varied but common design objectives: lightness, ease of use, and accessibility. New kitchens opt for functional elements, making them practical spaces with a rational distribution based on the differentiation of use. There are modules created exclusively for the cooking zone, the work zone, the pantry zone, or the storage area. Each zone may function independently, though all of them should be integrated with the entire kitchen ensemble. There is a wide range of designs on the market: ones with a retro tendency, ones of simple and pure line, or ones of industrial conception. Each kitchen acquires its own personality, and for this reason contemporary kitchen style incorporates a multitude of alternatives. Some options combine the most innovative materials while others tend toward more traditional materials. While many interior designers opt for light colors and the aesthetic of metallic materials such as stainless steel (which add luster and luminosity to the space), there are those who prefer bolder designs with colors such as red, intense yellow or blue, or dark wood fittings such as wengué. One of the essential characteristics of the contemporary home is the practicality of its elements. In many cases the kitchen is a kind of living room or an open area with a table that may serve for meals, studying, or work. Large spaces with an area reserved for the utility room or smaller kitchens in which the work area becomes a practical area for breakfasting are only some of the designs available for this room geared towards comfort, where originality is not reined in by merely practical function.

Design by: Massimo Iosa Ghini

Photography: Jordi Miralles

Photography: Jordi Miralles

Photography: Jörg Hempel

Design by: Elmar Cucine

ORIGINAL IDEA

Photography: José Luis Hausmann

WITH A VIEW

Design by: Massimo Iosa Ghini

Photography: José Luis Hausmann

MINIMALIST

Of pure conception and eclectic style, minimalist kitchens are noteworthy for occupying a single space in original environments without ornamental frills. Their clean and ordered forms constitute a decorative function. This type of kitchen tends to appear in new-style homes such as lofts or small studios in which the kitchen seeks to establish a unifying dialogue with the other areas of the home. They are kitchens of refined design, conceived to be functional while at the same time spectacular. Sometimes one wall contains all cabinets and kitchen elements thanks to an intelligent arrangement. Other times a single elongated module (island-fashion without separations) includes the kitchen, with all necessities reduced to a minimum of expression. In still another instance the kitchen shares space with the dining room and living room, requiring a rational, well-thought-out spatial arrangement. In homes without walls, the kitchen may be separated from the other rooms by panels of medium height. If the kitchen joins with other environments, furnishings in accord with the general decoration are required: light-toned furniture or dark cabinets to match the living room design are two possibilities. Some minimalist kitchens adapt to unconventional architectures, taking advantage of difficult angles, narrow corridors, or even sharing the same room with more than one environment. In minimalist kitchens the selection of contemporary materials for coverings and countertops combines with state-of-the-art domestic appliances to create an environment in which order and functionality are the two essential elements.

Photography: Andreas J. Focke

Photography: Elmar Cucine

Photography: Leon Chew

Photography: David M. Joseph

Photography: César San Millán

Photography: Nacása & Partners Inc.

A small kitchen demands an intelligent arrangement in order to take maximum advantage of a limited amount of available space. It is thus essential to achieve practical angles, columns, and corners. If a complete renovation is not possible, there are certain practical tricks that can be used. For example, sliding doors create space and permit the unification or separation of environments, given the necessities of the moment. Shelves or small cabinets to store utensils may be placed in corners or "dead zones." Most important, the kitchen must always be organized and permit easy movement regardless of limited surface area. Selecting fittings appropriate for this sort of kitchen is essential. Utilizing customized furniture is a good solution. Selecting auxiliary modules or furniture pieces with wheels is also a versatile option given that they can be moved, thus allowing space to be opened up when necessary. These pieces may be placed below the work table or utility-room table. The best alternative is to make use of walls to situate floor and ceiling cabinets (the latter may even reach the ceiling) in order to have enough storage space. Choosing light-colored furniture is wise for small kitchens, since they make the space seem larger. Any imaginative solution is appropriate, such as utilizing the space between steps in a set of stairs to store small items, hanging shelves from the ceiling to store cookbooks or work utensils, or making use of the kitchen sink for essentials while cooking. There are domestic appliances of reduced size, extendable exhaust hoods that occupy little space, and sinks and fixtures of simple design, all of which are ideal for this type of kitchen.

Photography: Montse Garriga

Photography: Carlos Domínguez

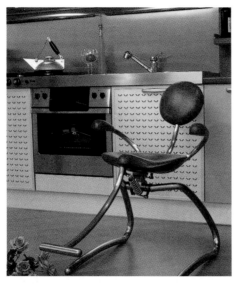

Photography: Eugeni Pons

Photography: Jordi Miralles

# INDUSTRIAL

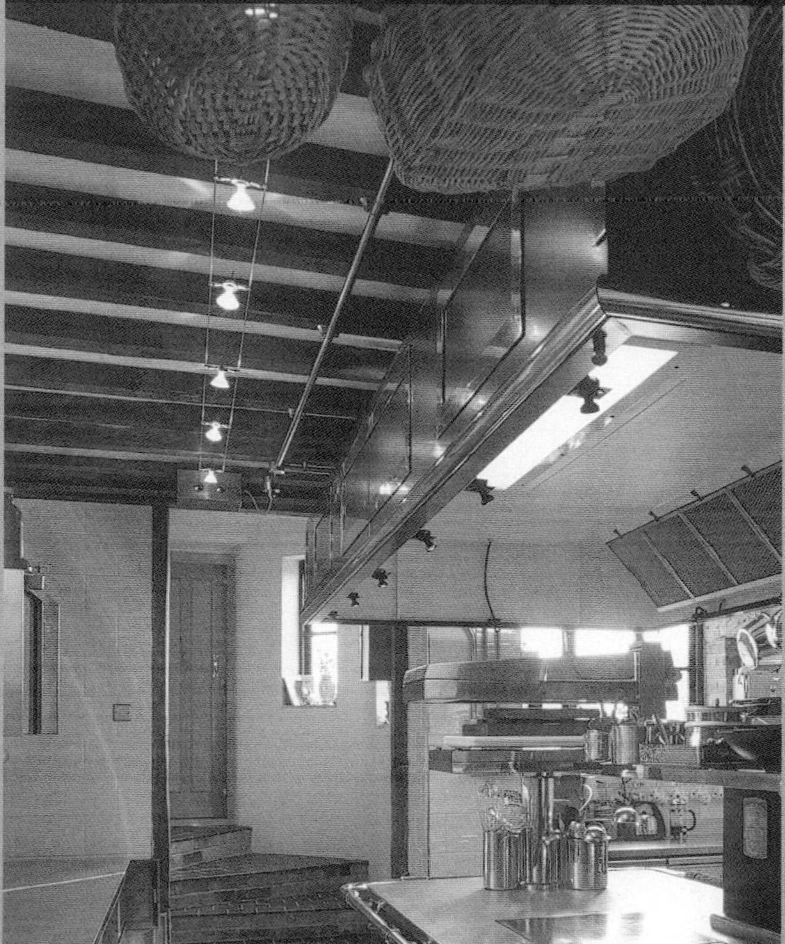

Nowadays, the distinctive style of kitchens in public places such as large restaurants is being imitated in many domestic settings. These are roomy, practical, well-thought-out spaces in which spatial distribution is centered on the activities of preparing and cooking meals. Stainless steel is usually employed in this type of kitchen, as it may be cleaned easily and is highly resistant to water vapor and grease. The majority of industrial kitchens are manufactured exclusively with this material. These designs have been adopted primarily in private homes where the culinary art figures largely. Increasingly, companies are manufacturing stainless steel cabinets, countertops, and hoods to match a gamut of up-to-date domestic appliances, sinks, and decorative elements. As a general rule, domestic appliances in this type of kitchen have a professional appearance and are of stainless steel to match the rest of the kitchen. Contemporary industrial kitchens follow avant-garde guidelines in which the space dedicated to cooking opens up to the other rooms. The tendency is to leave the work zone open to view and not relegate it to a secondary status. Some industrial kitchens, therefore, open to the restaurant with the aim of incorporating the preparation and enjoyment of meals in the same space. These kitchens incorporate refined designs with state-of-the-art materials that resist heat and chemical products. They are large, well-defined spaces with ample light. Distinct points of light in each zone allow one to work comfortably.

Photography: Eugeni Pons

## REINVENTING TRADITION

Photography: Carlos Domínguez

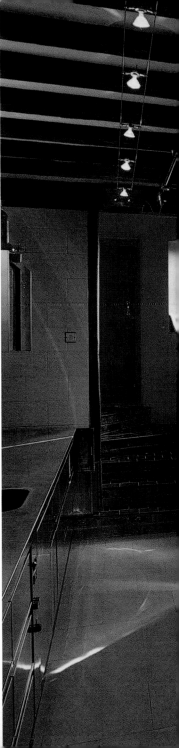

# ACCESSORIES